THE DAY BOOK

TED SMART

This edition produced by Ted Smart for
The Book People Ltd,
Guardian House,
Borough Road,
Godalming,
Surrey GU7 2AE

ISBN 1-85613-076-2

Manufactured in Spain

**Featuring the photography
of Christel Rosenfeld**

Produced by Ted Smart
Designed by Sara Cooper
Production Assistant : Seni Glaister

This book belongs to

SIGNS OF THE ZODIAC

AQUARIUS
January 21 – February 19

PISCES
February 20 – March 20

ARIES
March 21 – April 20

TAURUS
April 21 – May 21

GEMINI
May 22 – June 21

CANCER
June 22 – July 23

LEO
July 24 – August 23

VIRGO
August 24 – September 23

LIBRA
September 24 – October 23

SCORPIO
October 24 – November 22

SAGITTARIUS
November 23 – December 22

CAPRICORN
December 23 – January 20

JANUARY

JANUARY

1

2

3

4

5

6

JANUARY

7

8

9

10

11

12

JANUARY

13

14

15

16

17

18

JANUARY

19

20

21

22

23

24

JANUARY

25

26

27

28

29

30/31

FEBRUARY

FEBRUARY

1

2

3

4

5

6

FEBRUARY

7

8

9

10

11

12

FEBRUARY

13

14

15

16

17

18

FEBRUARY

19

20

21

22

23

24

FEBRUARY

25

26

27

28

29

MARCH

MARCH

1

2

3

4

5

6

MARCH

7

8

9

10

11

12

MARCH

13

14

15

16

17

18

MARCH

19

20

21

22

23

24

MARCH

25

26

27

28

29

30/31

APRIL

APRIL

1

2

3

4

5

6

APRIL

7

8

9

10

11

12

APRIL

13

14

15

16

17

18

APRIL

19

20

21

22

23

24

APRIL

25

26

27

28

29

30

MAY

MAY

1

2

3

4

5

6

MAY

7

8

9

10

11

12

MAY

13

14

15

16

17

18

MAY

19

20

21

22

23

24

MAY

25

26

27

28

29

30/31

JUNE

JUNE

1

2

3

4

5

6

JUNE

7

8

9

10

11

12

JUNE

13

14

15

16

17

18

JUNE

19

20

21

22

23

24

JUNE

25

26

27

28

29

30

JULY

JULY

1

2

3

4

5

6

JULY

7

8

9

10

11

12

JULY

13

14

15

16

17

18

JULY

19

20

21

22

23

24

JULY

25

26

27

28

29

30/31

AUGUST

AUGUST

1

2

3

4

5

6

AUGUST

7

8

9

10

11

12

21

AUGUST

13

14

15

16

17

18

AUGUST

19

20

21

22

23

24

AUGUST

25

26

27

28

29

30/31

SEPTEMBER

SEPTEMBER

1

2

3

4

5

6

SEPTEMBER

7

8

9

10

11

12

SEPTEMBER

13

14

15

16

17

18

SEPTEMBER

19

20

21

22

23

24

SEPTEMBER

25

26

27

28

29

30

OCTOBER

OCTOBER

1

2

3

4

5

6

OCTOBER

7

8

9

10

11

12

OCTOBER

13

14

15

16

17

18

OCTOBER

19

20

21

22

23

24

OCTOBER

25

26

27

28

29

30/31

NOVEMBER

NOVEMBER

1

2

3

4

5

6

NOVEMBER

7

8

9

10

11

12

NOVEMBER

13

14

15

16

17

18

NOVEMBER

19

20

21

22

23

24

NOVEMBER

25

26

27

28

29

30

DECEMBER

DECEMBER

1

2

3

4

5

6

DECEMBER

7

8

9

10

11

12

DECEMBER

13

14

15

16

17

18

DECEMBER

19

20

21

22

23

24

DECEMBER

25

26

27

28

29

30/31